Tuscaloosa
Grief Factory

Tuscaloosa Grief Factory

A.M. O'Malley

HUM
MING
BIRD
HEA
RT

LIMIT ZERO Publications
Portland, Oregon

LIMIT ZERO

PUBLICATIONS

This book is published by LIMIT ZERO Publications
www.LMTzero.com

Book Layout and Cover Design by
Olivia M. Hammerman, ochbookdesign.com

Cover photograph by Grant Gerald Miller

Published in the United States of America

ISBN 978-1-938753-52-7

"I'm no more your mother /
Than the cloud that distills
a mirror to reflect its own slow /
Effacement at the wind's hand."

—Sylvia Plath, "Morning Song"

The ghost watched over the curtain as the doctor cut me from hip to hip, a wave of bright red blood overflowed and spilled onto the floor. Everyone was very calm, chatting about the crimson tide. *Roll Tide Roll.* 'Bama football was the most sacred. I had never felt more alone. I had not known, until that moment, what a lonely experience it is to be in danger. I laid there staring at the sheet hung from the ceiling, *How did I get here?* My hand floated up and a hand came from behind and held it—I never learned whose. I watched the ghost's masked face as he watched the men dig around in the cave of my body and pull out what was not a hummingbird, but a human boy covered in his own black and yellow shit. *Meconium happens.* I felt my body rocked and saw a drop of my own blood on the floor. I waited behind the curtain like a performer in the wings. Matrescence is the word for becoming a mother, it is a death and a birth in one moment.

**

We drove south and east in a truck the color of a mustard seed with everything I had built inside. My feet swelled into pink distended squares with tiny toes sewn on. Four beating hearts—the little dog, the hummingbird moving in my belly, the ghost that I had married, and my own languid pulse. I struggled to catch my breath and we ate our way through America; Pendleton Casino Buffet, 31 flavors of ice cream in the desert, Chili's in Idaho, and one epic Taco Bell feast eaten from the shelf of my belly.

I learned the difference between the sound of a firework and the sound of a gunshot by moving to a thin-walled shack in Tuscaloosa, Alabama. Mid-summer in the Dirty South, flared and flattened and squashed like a spent cherry bomb.

I was in almost total solitude, though the ghost circled the same house. We were in the same rooms but far apart. The ghost was my best friend for a long time—his hunched-over silhouette coming toward me used to fill me with a sense of deep contentment. We married and became parents, and he was floating in the kitchen making pork three ways and then he was floating in the bathroom fixing the running toilet. When I told him I was pregnant he said, "I love you," he said, "I'm glad it's you." We stayed in our separate rooms during the day and came together to eat what he cooked in the evening before watching documentaries about other decades until I went to bed with my boy. He was far away on the other side of the couch and almost always chipper and stopped looking at me. Sometimes I cried for hours. He stayed up late drinking beer and slept until late morning.

In the time between my mother's death and the birth I was waiting for, I laid pinned on my side to a bed floating in the sea of a room filled with every cruel word I said to her, the woman who birthed me. The floor sloped to the north, I felt a deep pull in that direction—the direction of my birth and her death.

In Tuscaloosa that summer, I forgot to think about the longest day of the year. The next day felt just as long. During the blurriest time of the day, I sat on top of my husband while he tried to watch *Diners, Drive-Ins, and Dives*, I angled my head to get him to look in my eyes. I put his hand on my moving, fecund belly. He said he couldn't feel anything from inside a small orange bottle of lithium, that everything felt like the sun's core. My flesh expanded beyond the walls of the thin-walled shack, my skin so taut that it became translucent, a road map of veins clearly visible. I tried again to catch his eye, but he rippled and faded into a shadowy orb and slowly rose over my head, radiating heat. I watched him float into the kitchen to make more biscuits. We were always hungry at different times, and I was always hungry.

Tuscaloosa is there at the grace of the river, Black Warrior, it swells and trickles as best as it can. We rode into town in the middle of 127 days of drought, the roots of the water oak could be seen twisting into the exposed banks. It was there at the riverbank that I saw a red-tailed hawk turn her head to glare at me—just like my mother used to in the mornings. I wended my way through town back to our little shack and dreamed that mother-hawk came to me, like the night. She sank down between the trees and pressed into my cool pillow. She put her hand on my mouth, put her mouth to my ear, and reminded me that survival is transient, the clock, the shoe, the book would all become a monument to my want, the whisper said that I became heavy with objects that would outlive me, heavy with a child that would bring me back to life.

The ghost drove my car and I watched out the window in wonder as we drove past the rows and rows of glossy co-eds like paper doll cutouts, scrubbed, and painted, marching through the liquid heat under a 'Bama sun that is like no other sun. The hummingbird in my belly rolled and I couldn't look away from the spectacle of long legs and bleached orifices.

I was blissfully invisible to the college kids behind the spectacle of my fruiting belly. When strangers did see me, they gazed at me with smug smiles, a proprietary approval for continuing the human race—an act I already felt guilty about.

Spiraling out from the town center, past a crisscross of railroad tracks, the town unfurls like a fiddlehead fern, cars move up onto lawns, windows crack, houses clapboard, porches sag, yards turn to creeping Charlie and crabgrass, dogs loosen from their chains, refuse adorns each curb in spontaneous sculptures.

My husband had turned into a ghost but still asked me every 15 minutes if I needed anything. He was my favorite ghost. He rubbed my back. He came home drunk and snored in my face until I went to sleep on the couch. He told me that he loved me. He got drunk at our baby shower. He sat in the front seat of my car and talked about not wanting to watch our baby suffer. *Life is suffering.* He said that he doesn't matter anymore. He said he's spent his whole life with women angry at him. He said, "Remember when we used to sit up late and recite poems and drink tequila and fuck?" My body had grown huge with his baby. I thought about sending him away. I had no job. No family money, no family. I loved him. He was my favorite person. We said *they is*—an inside joke that strung us together. When he was steady on his feet, when he was clearheaded, he was my best friend. I married him. He went on lithium. We kept on.

There was often broken glass glinting in my mother's hair in the years before she got clean. The mornings made unreasonable demands on her. Her hair went silver the year she finally quit the booze and the white powder and the wide drawer of weed. She dyed her hair with henna, and it became an aura the color of crimson crayon around her face. I knew her from before she got clean and my baby would never know her after, this made me take precautions he might never learn to take. How to keep myself safe, step around broken crockery, tune out the sound of thunder.

I had the miles counted between my dying mother and my own sleeping body: 1,748 miles. To fall asleep, one must pretend to be dead.

I could not stop reading news stories of young children orphaned, young children witnessing their own mother's death, freak accidents that killed children in front of their mothers. I went down long corridors exploring the stories I found. My lungs would expand in my chest and my heart would shrink into a tightly clenched fist. The hummingbird flopped in my belly, and I kept looking.

I learned about grief from a doll on the bed
was named Timmy, a cake was baked on an
unnamed baby's death and birthday. When
my uncle Tom went crazy my grandmother
said it was because he watched his older
brother die. The last time I saw my mother
she gave me the rosary that had been
wrapped around Timmy's hands at his wake.
I knew what grief looked like and I'd found
new shapes of grief and I was afraid to find
more and sometimes all you can do is laugh
on your way to the gallows.

When you were dying, I was sleeping. I whispered this to my mother 1,000 times a day. It's funny the things you end up feeling guilty about. I'd hurt many people by accident and on purpose but hardly ever thought about it. I hoped to spot my mother with the other ghosts but so far there was only one appearance in the distance of a dream. I was afraid to sit on the ground for fear I'd have to roll out from under the tree and then call for help like a tipped turtle. Do turtles call for help? It was cool under the thick foliage, so I squatted down and felt the seams of my body pull.

I felt an urgency to make the ghost solid again. I wanted to tell him, "You lie in the orange gaze of my memory, now. Under my earth eyes, I fondle the back of your neck, that dappled neck I shaved in a tiny bathroom. That neck I squeezed as hard as my small hands could. It is inside your pulsing neck that I remember: we are two hearts in a forest at the edge of a lake. We are wet confetti after game day. Roll Tide. We are grease on the wheels of forgetting something important. The emergency brake on this ride has burned out. Some night, while you sleep, I'll come back to you. I'll freshen up my drink in our white kitchen. I'll splash cold water on my face and then I'll kneel next to your mouth. I'll pull out all your breath until you wither into something small enough to carry. I'll keep you in my breast pocket, I'll pat it to make sure you're still there when I need you."

The last time I spoke to my mother, I sat on a front stoop in Tuscaloosa with my belly hanging down between my knees. My mother sat under her bird feeders in Northern Minnesota. I asked her to come to Alabama when the baby arrived. She said she hoped she would be feeling better by then. I thought she would. A cardinal landed close to my bare foot.

"That must be your grandmother," she said matter-of-factly. *"She wants to see that baby bump."*

We laughed. The cardinal hopped closer. It was cool for April in Alabama.

She said that white people don't say *swaddle*, but I don't remember what she called it, *bundling*? I rushed her off the phone because the ghost was making biscuits. She could say goodbye for days.

"Okay, I'm going to let you let me go too, Ma."

"Okay, bye honey ... Oh! Your grandfather always wanted to name a son Maximilian, but

your grandmother wouldn't let him, so he named a dog that—and it was a chihuahua!"

"Okay, bye Mom."

"Yes, you have to go … Oh! Rub wash cloths on your nipples to toughen them up for nursing!"

"Mom! I have to go. Bye." Click.

I went upstairs and ate biscuits with smears of salted butter and red raspberry jam. I never spoke to my mother again, though she wouldn't be dead for another 46 days. There was no good reason for this, I just thought she'd be there.

There are so many ways we carry those who have tried to love us, whether they succeeded or not. We carry their story into our own survival and there is a reckoning each day.

One night in the thin-walled Tuscaloosa shack the boy would not stop screaming. Before he was born, I took a class on the first weeks and the instructor told us we would learn to identify the type of cry from our newborns and what it would mean the baby needed. But all I could hear was *scream* and sometimes *wail*. The ghost rippled in the doorway and slammed through the house. In the morning I heard him mutter in the kitchen. *I almost made it; I was this close to being free.* He had his own ghosts.

We took the baby boy out into the world. He was weighed and measured. His body curled in on itself. His long fingers fanned against his own cheek. *Existing is plagiarism.* We went to the drive-through on the way home. The ghost wanted a footlong chili dog but didn't want any French fries. He leaned forward and spoke loudly into the speaker. *I want a chili dog, just the hot dog. Just the hot dog!* He didn't get what he wanted.

I whispered to my boy as he sucked from me, *You come from a long line of people watchers. You come from a long line of weak chins. You come from a long line of Wheel of Fortune. You come from a long line of drowning. You come from a long line of pencil sharpening. You come from a long line of Icehouse Beer. You come from a long line of ivy-patterned wallpaper. You come from a long line of chocolate chip cookies. You come from a long line of yellow shoes. Your skin is the skin I had. Your skin is half ghost.*

I pressed my face to the window. Cars drove past with bass that rattled the pane against my cheek. The thin shack was sealed up tight with cold air, but the press of the pure white heat outside warmed my mouth and chin. The ghost could be heard rattling the loose cabinet handle over the stove. I imagined my eyelashes could be singed off if I stood there against the glass long enough. I would become hollowed out and faceless with a milky boob and two arms left for the boy. The radio sang along with the ghost. Bacon spit. The boy stirred. The floor tilted up to meet me. Nothing is anything if you say it is.

When the baby boy was born the doctor said he was a stargazer—I emptied out with terror. I let the doctor cut through all eight layers of my guts and pull loose my confused stargazing baby, that was when my heart fell out of my chest and splashed on the floor. He wasn't really stuck—it was me who was stuck, suspended in water, gasping. Grief is carried in the hips. The hips must open to give birth. Grief is carried in the hips. The hips must open to give birth. Grief is carried in the hips. The hips must open to give birth.

Even if I knew that luck was a myth, I still knocked wood, consulted the stars, kept my fingers perpetually crossed. I spent most days hiding from luck in the smallest room of the thin-walled Tuscaloosa house. I wrapped the boy up in muslin, tied tight, mimicking the sardine can of my belly. He slept beside me, and I laid my hands lightly on my own face to recreate my mother's hands there.

The radio had become inhabited with a new ghost and only played one jingle, *Call 205 and seven 4s … 24/7 we'll be at your door! Freedom, heating, and cooling!* The ghost sang along on a loop that only stopped when he was pulling biscuits out of the oven. *Call 205 and seven 4s … 24/7 we'll be at your door! Freedom, heating, and cooling!* I felt myself evaporating and could not drink enough water. Sweat, blood, lochia, and milk leaked out of me. *Call 205 and seven 4s … 24/7 we'll be at your door! Freedom, heating, and cooling!* Freedom was out of reach and the cold inside air kept me locked in. The nights had always been long and easy to get lost in, but the days in Tuscaloosa sometimes went on for days.

A neon sign appeared one morning, buzzing over my head with the words DEAD MOTHER. I could not seem to remember to change my mother from *is* into *was*. I was wrapped in cotton batting muffling everything but the delighted intake of breath my mother would sound when she realized it was her only daughter calling her.

I walked through the days and fell into the nights. Washing clothes, bending, reaching, nursing, singing, breathing in and out, watching the loose dogs through the window. I sat on the splintered back stoop in the mornings with the baby boy in my arm, saltwater fell on his face. The water in my glass rippled when the ghost passed by me on the way to the car. The clouds emptied their water each afternoon in a frightening torrent. This pain was a wild thing, a hog on a leash, whipping me around, battering me against the walls. To hold on to it was not possible, but I kept trying anyway.

The butter had gone rancid again, on the kitchen counter, it made the toast taste like blue cheese. I ate it, anyway, chewing and listening to the trumpet kid out back. He was improving. The heat was a hand on my throat. The bottoms of my feet had gone hard, and I could walk over bottle caps without feeling anything. Late one afternoon, after I had shut myself and the boy inside against the sun, the little dog crawled under the darkest part of the magnolia tree. He curled into a tightly wound golden ratio and died from the smell of stale beer, oil slicks, and the common anguish of old age. The ghost buried him tenderly under a water oak by the river. I stayed home and leaked more saltwater into the damp head of the baby boy. I wondered if babies could feel loneliness. I whispered into the fontanelle, *We've got to live, no matter how many skies have fallen.* I'd read that somewhere but couldn't remember where.

Learning the trumpet, like getting a divorce,
is a real act of hope.

Some cicadas spend most of their lives as underground nymphs, emerging only after 15 years. They make their songs by beating themselves like drums. In Tuscaloosa the cicadas worked themselves ragged at dusk, a stadium sound of deep dense noise. I laid in the smallest room of the thin-walled Tuscaloosa house and read *The Diary of Anaïs Nin*, the boy attached and suckling at my life force. *We place blame on objects and people for holding us captive—but we are the ones who hold ourselves captive.* I closed my eyes and whispered into the boy's ear, *This noise will be the sound of home.*

The skin inside our mother's wrist, the space between her arms when she held me. I saw a doe that didn't know she was about to die. What would I have said if I had known it would be the last thing I would say? Once I found triplet fawns in a highway median. They were speckled and small. I called the police and the man on the other end of the phone said, *Nothing to be done but let them die*, so I did. I let my mother die. I didn't let my boy die. A cesarean is an act of love.

I was looking for my mother in Tuscaloosa's oldest tree. I started driving to try to find a wild place, but the south had been broken-in like an old pair of boots for too long and there are few wild places left in our patch of Alabama. I found the Black Warrior River again behind a barricade of crepe myrtle, rose bushes, and concrete but couldn't get down to the water's edge. I found an old golf course, choked with kudzu and wailing with those faithful cicadas, and it felt close to wild there, close to my mother. I walked there for hours each day with the baby boy strapped to my body, both of us wet with sweat. My umbrella-sized sun hat covered us both. I didn't know what it was until I found it.

It's impossible to know how many ways we'll fail our children. My mother used to make me sandwiches when I was a small child. Before she gave them to me, she almost always took a round bite out first. When I grew up my rage could not be stopped, and those sandwiches became proof that she never thought of me as a person.

I threw biscuit crusts out back next to the magnolia tree hoping for cardinals to arrive. I needed to send some questions with them to my mother. *Why the fuck did you have to die when you did? Where is your body? Were you spoon-fed sips of water? Did your husband whisper my son's name into your ear to wake you? Why wasn't that enough?* The cardinals arrived, one dun and one vivid as my last memory of speaking to my mother. I gave them my questions and thought about my mother's last words of advice, *Rub your nipples with a rough cloth to prepare for nursing.* The baby boy rode the crest of my leaking chest with an expression of complete dissatisfaction, his brow crumpled and complaining like an old love note. His eyelashes reached for me like hands.

The ghost left me each day early in the morning, leaving behind one-handed snacks, extra ice in the freezer, stacks of clean diapers within reach, fresh pitchers of water. I stared at the door when it shut behind him and started the countdown of hours alone with the boy. The thin-walled Tuscaloosa house held us both like a lace glove, letting in the sounds of barking dogs, the smell of grills lit with spurting accelerants, the persistent, continual, never-ending, relentless, droning, uninterrupted sun. I wandered from room to room with the boy tied to my chest, cutting the day into little scraps, and then cutting them again into smaller scraps. When the ghost came home, I conjured up something to tell him about our day. *The floors in this house all slope in a different direction.*

I watched women at the grocery stores wheeling carts of children, other mothers pulling toddlers out of seats, pushing them into other seats. I closed my eyes and they all floated in front of me; women, mothers, getting dressed, going on diets, going to work, staying home, nursing, pelvic floors falling, trying to please their daddy ghosts. *How does everyone do this when it is completely impossible to do? Was it the death of my mother and the birth of my child, the two most impossible things crammed together in one long summer like the tails of two snakes tied together?* I carried 1,000 plastic sacks of groceries into the thin-walled shack, the baby boy screamed from his car seat with desperate hunger, a line of lochia tracked down my leg. A yard of shirtless men watched me from across the street. A photograph of my young mother roundly pregnant with a nimbus of dark hair and ski-jump nose, a look of cloudless calm on her face, a cigarette between her first and second finger was pinned to my wall. A good enough mother is good enough except for when she isn't.

The baby boy is an egg on the sidewalks of Tuscaloosa, buckled and uneven with jagged broken waves of concrete waiting to crack him. I walked with him up and down the shady side of the street, anxiety tickling the length of my spine, wondering how I would manage to ever let him out in the world on his own. A new worry crashed over me with each step, *When will my boobs stop aching? When will my belly feel less like an empty sack, loose and stitched into a wide ghoulish grin? What if the boy has some illness I can't see? Do the vibrations of thumping cars give him nightmares?* I was blind with these thoughts, marching into the setting sun when a car slowed down beside me and the sleeping boy in his stroller. *Are you married?* A man slung low in the front seat of a matte-colored muscle car, dips his chin at me. I am confused by his question and gape at him for possibly an hour, possibly 30 seconds. *Yes.* I can finally say. *What a shame.* He dipped his chin again and drove on by. *What a shame.* The phrase feels like a smooth cool pebble under my tongue.

My mother always called me at the wrong time, said the wrong thing, and cried louder than me. *I'm tired, Mom. WELL, WE'RE ALL TIRED.* The day I left home on a Greyhound I was seventeen and stuffed taut with hot daughter rage. My mother drove fast ahead of the bus on the highway, she parked again on the crest of a hill, jumped out to watch me leave again. She didn't see me wave back.

I was taught you can't hate the dead. I hated my mother for her sudden death after 17 years of dying. I hated my mother for her inability to tell our flesh apart. I hated my mother for giving birth into a world that has 150 states of being but all of them suffering. I couldn't bring myself to believe in heaven or hell, but I believed in dust and, in that way, I knew I would be with my mother again, when we were both just motes under a bed or on the ass of a horse. We'd be together then. I could hate her while holding her hand.

The baby boy's stomach is the size of a marble. If baby can't latch, hand express into a teaspoon to give to him. *Don't lose a drop of colostrum. Look for smacking lips, tongue out. Is baby swallowing? Do you hear the sound of the milk? Output, meconium looks like black tar. Then, it should be green but not too green. Look for mustard yellow. To burp or not to burp. Pay attention to the latch. Practice drowsy but awake. Recreate the womb. When will baby sleep through the night?* The waking every hour with the baby boy dulled me into a blunt object. There was no way to see to the bottom of need at 2am.

Then there were moments of the craziest all-encompassing joy. When I was 20 and got my first puppy. I took her to the park to play. While watching her frolic and jump I felt a strange cracking open sensation in my chest and thought, *This is love*. Years later I felt it with the ghost multiplied by 10. With the baby boy this sensation was repeated and magnified 300 times each mindless endless day. He was mine as nothing and no one had ever been mine. His face, his feet, his flailing legs, the inside of his mouth, his shit, his vomit—all mine. There was a bubble and he and I were in it. The rest of the room, the thin-walled Tuscaloosa house, the ghost, the cracked sidewalk, the clover, the water oak, the burning surface of the sun were all muted, meaningless, and blurred outside of *us*. It was just us. I was erased.

With a panic I realized that I was running the risk of forgetting he was a person separate from me, that I would forget to let him be. As my mother forgot, and now it was too late to forgive her for another thing. I watched other mothers, their knees buckled under this weight. I watched them carefully, some seemed to deal by attempting to micromanage; some went crazy; some zoned out. Or all of the above. The trick is to surrender completely, don't dare want for more.

Sometimes in the long afternoons when there were too many hours until bedtime, I nursed my son to quiet him, his head fit just below the tattoo on my arm that said, "MOM." My mother used to ask to look at it and I would lift my arm and splay out the inner soft bit for her to see clearly the thin red heart with simple rays and red-inked word. I would turn my arm upside down and we'd both exclaim "WOW" and when we laughed together, I felt our blood. Now that tender ink is as close as I can get to his soft face, some of the rays have worn off from the sun but the word "MOM" still burns bright. I want to see her, see me as a mother, with my breast in the mouth of my long lean boy.

The ghost spent each day teaching co-eds
about *Sir Gawain and the Green Knight* and
the oxford comma, but we were running out
of money. I found a job working a few hours
a week at the library on the wrong side of
town. I handed the baby boy to the ghost
and took my still eviscerated leaking body
to work. The woman who trained me on
checking books in and out and how to log
people on to computers only had one eye
and a thick Alabama drawl. She said I still
looked pregnant. During my first shift, my
boobs became two squares of concrete in
my blouse. An elderly woman came in to
pay her grandson's library fines with money
she pulled from her bra—the one-eyed lady
set the money aside and put a post-it on it
that said, "BOOB MONEY." *I like to let it
air out.* I locked myself in the bathroom to
pump milk into a bottle and tally how many
dollars I have earned.

There was no funeral, no death ritual. I just heard the news via Facebook Messenger. An uncle wrote, "Condolences," and I knew she had died. She gave me a song to play. She wanted bagpipes. But her ashes are locked in a closet at the funeral home because the stepfather drank the money we gave him to pay for her ashes. He drank handles of vodka and called my mother's best friend Diane, but she hung up on him as soon as she could hear that he'd been drinking. The night before my mother died, Diane called, and he placed the phone by my mother's head. Diane said her goodbyes to the sound of my mother's labored breath and when my mother's husband put the phone to his ear Diane said, *"Goodbye, you puke."*

I called my mother's best friend Diane on my mother's birthday. She told me how they were supposed to get their tonsils out together when they were teenagers. They were going to share a room and eat popsicles and watch TV but on the day of the surgery, Diane got mono and had to go to a different wing and my mother got her tonsils out alone. I called my mother's sister and she talked nonstop like she was on something fast, which is not beyond the realm of possibility. I called my mother's favorite brother and he had forgotten it was his dead sister's birthday.

I remembered as a child what it felt like to wait for my mother to come home. When I was five, she told me to never answer the phone and to lay flat on the ground if someone came to the door. She worked at the grocery store and as a maid and as a welder and selling Amway. I watch my baby boy play alone on the floor of his room, he is still a flowerpot, not crawling and I want to fix all of his troubles. A snowplow for him forever.

My mother used to say, "You're my pumpkin pie," and I would say it back. She would say, "You're my strawberry shortcake." She always had a sweet tooth. I prefer the taste of salt. My mother hollowed me out and made me hungry. I remember the shape of her mouth spooning heaping mounds of vanilla ice cream, Cheerios, and milk into her mouth. Her body disgusted me. The sound of milk thick in her throat disgusted me. There are no places inside me that are not changed or made by her. I studied her loose stretch-marked apron belly and swinging breasts in the shower. My body has become her body—stretched out and sucked on by my own child. I held my belly in the shower, it puckered and filled my hands. I say, "I love you." I held my sorrow in my belly, I sucked it in, punched at it, pinched it. I watched all the naked women of my family do the same. I inherited a habit of laughing when I should cry—all that pain really can be funny but some of our stories have had to shift because they aren't funny anymore.

In my memory, my stepfather just arrived one day. My mother said an old friend, *oldest friend*, was coming to call. He came after dark with his own mother, and they sat quietly in our living room. I didn't know we were in the eye of a cyclone. Our singlewide trailer had only seen one birthday party since mother got clean. There was a banner, a sheet cake, balloons on the mailbox. The stepfather's mother had legs like freshly pulled taffy. I watched them the whole evening.

My son has a father, the ghost, a tall lean man with long eyelashes. The ghost cut back on smoking, he soothed and rocked the baby boy every night, cooked us all dinners with bright herbs and thick sauces. Yes, he turned into a ghost but where I come from all fathers are ghosts.

A drunk driver killed our uncle when he was checking the mail. He was nine and had blue eyes like my boy. When I lived past nine years, I breathed a sigh of relief. When my baby brother was nine, he loved the neighbor's dog so much he sometimes ran away to visit her. We could keep him then. Our mother could pull him back from anything but by then I wasn't there anymore.

I go back and forth between present and past tense. She was, she is. You were, you are. I always just am. I am, I am. It's been 302 days since she died. It's been 348 days since I talked to our mother. It's been 1,453 days since she died. It's been 1,499 days since I talked to our mother. It has been 1,952 days since she died. It has been 1,998 days since I last talked to our mother. I can sometimes only think of her as my mother, only mine—but she was your mother too.

My mother finally visited me in the form
of a red cardinal all this winter. *Hi Mom.*
I pointed her out to the baby boy, and he
screeched.

I tell the baby boy to remember arrows, like birds, need feathers to fly. I must believe that he will fly and that one night we will sit together like friends. Snow will fall, he will get up to put on old boots. Outside, he will drag a plastic sled to the woodpile with the dogs dancing around him. I will watch from the window as his back bends to the work of the wood. I will bring him back through the snow with my watching, back from the cord of wood, back from the hanging ice, the bottomless dusk.

At the center, Tuscaloosa is a college town with a true religion of football, a chorus of *Roll Tide*, rich white kids in giant Jeep Wranglers, wind in their halos, and sprawling Greek houses with their milk-colored columns bringing us all closer to God. Polo shirts, duck boots, and khaki pants the uniforms for the boys, long Señor Frog T-shirts over short short slick slippery shorts and long looking-glass hair for the girls.

I walked out again, eyes on a swivel for loose dogs, I went slowly through the neighborhood with my little dog. His tongue rolled out and became our herald as we sailed along together. My belly was an ambassador—people came out of their houses to bless us; they laughed and shook their heads. They exclaimed over my imminent motherhood. "That baby is gonna fall out." "Not long now!" "You gonna pop, mama." "What you having?" I nodded and smiled and kept walking in my new slow waddle, my body pitched and yawed side to side threatening to topple.

Sometime, just after she died, I felt that my dead mother had moved into my chest, crowded against the baby in my belly. When I closed my eyes, I saw her lying on her deathbed. There had never been a world without her.

I laid in the smallest darkest room in the thin-walled house and dreamed I was reaching into my own vagina and pulling my baby out quickly before he had time to drown. This dream comes every night and each time I pulled the small bloody body to my chest, it was my mother in my arms.

In Tuscaloosa, at the molten core of the day we got into the car to buy food. I lost my breath in the stuffed heat of the front seat. The ghost and I didn't look at each other, just out the windows as the tightly-boxed buildings of Tuscaloosa flew past. We parked at Target. The produce section gave me a choking sensation—like the baby's foot was pressing up on my lungs. The vegetables lined up sparse and old reminded me of my days in the food deserts of my childhood. Limp spring mix, baby carrots loose with slime, red delicious apples waxy and two-dimensional. The ghost stalked the aisles with his list, and I skidded along after him like a water skier on a shiny lake. This was the best we could do there.

I laid in a wide bed in Tuscaloosa and played these tapes over and over in the forced-air loneliness of the afternoons. I visualized my hummingbird being born into a boy, I visualized his dirty elbows, bent toenails, his quick breath, his mouth suckling. I wanted to skip over the birth part. My dreams tried to solve all my worries and I woke up with a start and disappointment that I still had the hummingbird inside me. Getting birthed is like driving a stick shift: ease off the brake and clutch and push in on the gas.

I tried to fall in love with the birds in
Alabama. So much of everything looked the
same to me. The heat kept me inside. When
I went out, I felt surrounded by garbage and
cars driving too close to the sidewalk and
disease-carrying mosquitoes and ticks and
packs of uncut dogs and menacing snakes.
The sound of the cicadas was violent. I
mostly stayed inside, evaporating in the air
conditioning, apologizing silently to the
little dog I brought out here.

I wanted to tell my mom that our bodies are naïve. Our tongues move food into the places between our teeth. Our tongues are not afraid of being bitten and they are bitten all the time. My baby brother cried for months. My mother was furious at how things had been handled. The break between air and no air means a life of difference. I was different and I looked the same—nothing to tell the tale of the rough passage of birth.

I had a body, but it was replaced with a packed honeycomb. I tucked myself into bed at night with five hundred pillows strategically placed and wished I could take it all back before drifting off to sleep.

I wanted to tell my mother that knowing her was like not feeling hungry until I took the first bite. I held the boy in the air-conditioned afternoons thinking of when my mother needed to fold her wings and turn into a dove.

I read about gravediggers looking for valuable confederate memorabilia. An old man digging up his wife. A man on TV burying his shark-bitten lover. When I die, I want my flesh to rot. I walked to the oldest cemetery in Alabama and saw cake-pan gravestones of young children. I thought about skeletons found with their hands pounding the tops of their coffins.

I laid awake in the wide bed at night terrified
that my hummingbird would die in the silk
purse of my womb. That my unproven pelvis
would prove faulty and drown him before he
could surface with a wail.

I wrote a plan. *Birth ball, squat bar, tub, shower, birth stool, wireless monitor, peanut ball, episiotomy, forceps, vacuum. Rooming in. Microbiome. Vernix on crow's feet. Wait to cut the cord.* I wrote these on a piece of paper and that is where they stayed.

The ghost's skin became a map folded and refolded, lines creased in a singlewide, high desert next to me on the mattress.

I passed a woman while walking in the woods. She looked at me and said, "Yes."

Yes to the fact that we are passing, that we are women in the world alone in the woods? Yes to the heat? The clear morning? My obvious bringing of life?

"Yes," I said back.

Stray dogs with testicles dangling between their back legs trotted through the streets. People parked their cars on their lawns. Every house on our street had a "No Trespassing" sign. Cars didn't slow down when I attempted to scuttle my huge pregnant body and my little dog across the wide streets. The doctor's office was a Kafkaesque nightmare where they never said my name the same way twice and the ghost and I sat and waited and didn't talk to each other for hours. I was usually crying by dinnertime.

I was almost always hopeful in the morning.
I couldn't stop the rush of hope flooding in.
It wasn't until the late afternoon that the
darkness came. The boy cried each day from
3pm to 6pm.

The sound of a gun is hollow, like the echo of one's own voice.

My fondest wish had always been to be
different, to stand out, to somehow be seen.
For the freshmen of Tuscaloosa, it appeared
that variation on the chosen uniform was
punishable by social annihilation. I got
out of our little house and wandered the
streets sipping a too-sweet coffee. I looked
and looked and could find no recognizable
difference between the center of the town
and a fresh pack of peppermint gum—
pristine in its neatness.

That is where we found our place—our thin-walled shack. Where I came to give birth not knowing a soul except for the ghost. Where I prowled from window to window, my little hummingbird always moving inside me, where I spent heat-soaked days willing the outside, the swelter, the Greek, and the drawling voices to stay outside.

My mother's stories have now become my stories. I dole them out as best I can. Each time I get something wrong.

While we were living apart, before the moving hummingbird, before my mother died, my ghost—who was not yet a ghost— and I texted each other several times an hour. He had his own chime and each time it rang a thrill ran from the crown of my head to the tip of my clit. We sent the same phrases over and over.

They is.

I choose you today.

I love the shit outta you.

Existing is plagiarism.

We wrote poems back and forth, FaceTime fucked, talked of our love a total eclipse.

In those first keening postmortem days each time I closed my eyes I saw the painting that hung in the back of my mind; Magritte's painting *The Lovers*, two heads wrapped in white cloth kissing. When Magritte was thirteen, his mother committed suicide by drowning herself in a river. When she was found, her nightgown was wrapped around her head.

I wanted to tell my mother that since we were born our friendship with Death has been a long and easy one. The two of us held hands with Death in the park. We would swing on the swings, laugh together at the graffitied picnic table. But I got jealous, I want to steal her back from Death, but please don't tell Death I said that. I wanted a piece of my mother's hair. I wanted her to show me what the world says. I want to hang a sign over my son's head that says in block print, "BE CAREFUL."

I held my fresh baby boy and tried to remember the face of the first man who touched me. I could remember his ripped collar and the hard way he pushed at me and in me. My legs were brown sticks and coated in red clay dust from the long walk to his house. I told everyone I met that I was as old as they were. I walked to the 7-Eleven to make a call after sneaking out of the boy's house, my mother came to get me. She knew something had happened, so she took me to TCBY for some frozen yogurt. That red clay dust clung to my shoes for years.

The ghost whispered about Schopenhauer. I changed the channel from McConaughey's scraggle to Mountain Dew in the shape of a man. The ghost made a joke about making do. The boy was too pink, a cooked shrimp in the bed of my arm. I fussed over keeping the sun off of him, but the sun always won and had burned several holes in the boy until he was riddled. The ghost murmured about the sins of the father, and I ordered a sun hat as big as an umbrella.

My birds refused to land in the yard at the same time. They flew in circles above the lawn. My mother had not seen where I slept since 1998. The trees laugh at these problems, and people cut them down. My mother and I were sewn together with a jagged seam. We were far apart but our dreams called each other collect.

I need a mnemonic device to remember how
to breathe without a mother in the world.
Sometimes you breathe for your child, and
they never find out until you're gone.

The thin-walled shack sat between a church where the congregants wore all white and a dirt yard of shirtless men. On Sundays the church took over the sound of the street. It pulsed and vibrated with those brilliant bodies. Tambourines, clapping hands, and voices rose, waking the boy from his morning nap. I lifted him from his bed, settled him to my nipple, and sat on the floor closest to the window. I swayed back and forth, closed my eyes, and hummed into the swirl of his scalp, as if I belonged somewhere like that.

My mother died holding her husband's hand. Every time I spoke to my mother for the last fifteen years of her life, she told me she was going to leave him, she was going to get a divorce, she was going to get in her truck and drive away and never look back—instead she died with her hand in his. I found out she had slipped into a coma because she wasn't posting on Facebook and her oldest friend got concerned. It turned out that my mother swore everyone to secrecy about her deteriorating health. She didn't want me to be upset with a baby in my belly, so she took away my goodbye.

I wanted to tell my mother, *Mom, you will never read this. You will never trace your finger on these words, but if you do—I'm sorry I escaped before we could find out what makes the other laugh. You knew me before I had feet. I see my own little kicking legs in the little kicking legs of my boy. When you laughed, I looked behind me. When you laughed, I retraced my steps. I have a blinded version of you. I mortar together the parts we share, tie us together with strings strung by your mother and her mother—we could have easily become strangers and I tried to make you a stranger and I failed.*

The day became a wheel instead of a coin. Light and night swirled into each other. I got to know the small circle of light on the wall at 3am as I moved from bed to couch to bed to couch. I became dependent on a contraption called My Breast Friend which buckled around my body to keep the boy in position. Milk. To milk is to bleed. To milk is to take advantage of. To milk is to squeeze. To milk is to fleece. The milk tasted like the bottom of a cereal bowl. I woke up in a pool of sticky milk. Lazy boob. Boob flu. Mastitis. Liquid gold. I held an electric toothbrush to my breast. There is no such thing as a clogged boob. I got on all fours and placed the boy under me, hoping he would suck the pain out through my nipple. He split into his first spasmodic smile, windmilled his limbs.

I fell asleep while eating. I fell asleep while walking. I fell asleep while nursing. I never slept, only fell.

I arrived in Tuscaloosa in an advanced state of pregnancy one week after my mother died.

I have so many things to say to no one in particular, because my mother is dead and the hummingbird in my belly can't hear me over the monotonous singing in my veins. I never learned that it's not the horror of war people are interested in. It's how worn their own shoes are. How large their bodies have become. Whether or not to watch one more episode. People don't remember death the way my mother did. She came close enough to it that it never left her. My mother isn't on this earth anymore—but she is. She is burned and bagged at the funeral home until we come up with the money to claim her ashes. My baby could have met our mother when she was old. I met our mother when she was a child—but never had much more of her in the end.

I had assumed my mother would continue to survive. She had been shitting white and leaving orange residue on her clothes for years—chronic and persistent liver failure. She lasted longer than any of us thought she would and left so suddenly we couldn't catch up to say goodbye.

Sometimes I marveled that I had been in her body, the same body was now rotting somewhere, waiting to be burned to ash or already burned to ash and in a bag on a shelf waiting to be picked up. Her cells and her mother's cells, my Emeraude perfume-smelling grandmother, were still floating around in my body too. Maternal micro chimerism is all I have left of their living bodies.

I comforted myself thinking I was a chimera
in my baby's blood. I had burned to ash with
my mother. I bled my mother out on my
12th birthday. She flooded the white cotton
of my unsuspecting underwear.

The men around when she died, brothers,
husband, uncles, swinging dicks aplenty,
they all said that she didn't want a funeral.
Nothing I could do from 2,000 miles away,
about to pop out a boy-hummingbird. But
I have a memory of a hot phone pressed
to my ear, pacing outside in my front yard
while my mother told me she wanted
"Amazing Grace" on the bagpipes.

I closed my eyes in the thin-walled shack and I could see the hair on her nape. She loved to mow the lawn. She sweated in rivulets, hair curled around her face. I could see her hands. I took pictures of her hands next to mine. We would marvel at how our hands looked exactly the same—small, square with square flat fingernails. Our hands resembled each other more closely than our faces. I didn't take enough pictures of her legs, also twins to mine—tree trunks of power with curving calves and small ankles. Both so proud of our ankles. Her nose was a sky jump, mine is a snowbank. Her eyes were a dark gray blue, like mine. What I would do for a lock of her wavy hair. I recorded her voice, but the recording came out muffled.

My mother and I were both pregnant in summer. We both held buzzing blond hummingbirds in our bellies through the swaying heat—she was in the desert; I was in the great American south. We both split open before spilling forth large boys.

I wanted to write to my mother because she died at the worst possible time, is there a best time for your mother to die? I can't help but think that she died when I was just on the verge of learning how much she loved me.

I wrote in a straight back chair, my lower back ached. My left butt cheek turned numb. Every few minutes a stinging pain would shoot down my right hip. My feet swollen. My toes were numb. My face was puffy. I had black hairs sprouting from my nipples and my chin. I couldn't shit. I needed to take a nap every afternoon. I hadn't seen my vulva for months. I couldn't sleep for more than four hours at a time. My thighs became mottled with cellulite. I had red burst blood vessels all over my chest. I loved the way my belly looked. My belly button was exposed to the world for the first time. My hair, soft and supple, and thick as it was when I was a child. I fantasized about lying on my stomach. I felt guilty for lying on my back for more than a few minutes. I ate at least one cheese Danish each day.

My mother lived in a three-room cabin in the most northern Minnesota woods. The roads around her house are slick much of the year. I imagined I could chain her to a safe place, away from any danger. *Stay close to home, Mom. Never stop eating salt and pepper on your pancakes. You didn't leave us until you had to.*

In Tuscaloosa, the thin-walled shack became crowded with ghosts. My dead grandmother was clucking her tongue at how my living ghost husband sliced the hard-boiled eggs. Faint as mist, I thought I spotted my mother floating near the ceiling—but it is another ghost, one I didn't know. I propped a photograph of my mother up next to my pillow, in it she is clutching a geology textbook. Will anyone else remember how much she loved rocks? I woke up and the house was finally empty.

Birth, death, motherhood all tight in a tightly mangled knot. I've never had the patience required for untangling the thin chains of necklaces at the bottom of my jewelry box.

I missed crossing my legs and felt guilty crossing my ankles—afraid my pelvis would become a locked door too. I fretted silently over my body becoming a cage for the little Houdini in my belly. I had a recording of his heartbeat, thundering hooves, I played the recording for my mother once and she gasped in delight. She knew his name. She heard his heart. *Breathe, breathe, beat, beat,* I whispered as a mantra into my own belly.

The thin-walled shack was surrounded. I heard squirrels dancing in the eaves, cats fighting under the porch. Through the blinds I watched as the neighbor, Cedric, built daily sculptures in his dirt yard of indigo blue Bud Light boxes and the refuse of fireworks. Thumping music wrung from the open cab of a hoodless truck. He sat on a cooler, drinking from the cans wrapped in koozies, and received shirtless visitors throughout the day like a tired king.

Sometimes, the sound of a wilting trumpet could be heard as it came through the thick foliage of the shiny magnolia out back. Bare brown feet of a large boy could be seen under the branches, one foot tapping to keep time. I watched from my spot on the rotting back deck, the backyard was mostly shrouded in bottle caps and the clinking boats of dropped magnolia leaves and his feet never acknowledged my listening. The hummingbird flew in my belly.

I was huge with my own boy hummingbird.
At night when I dreamt about the graceful,
fluid birth, my hummingbird's long limbs
sluicing out of me I woke up feeling as if
I had solved a troubling puzzle opened in
Chino Valley and never put back together.

The crystal ball was clear and high definition—my mother was dead. My mother died after many years of dying. My mother was gone. My mother was no longer with us. My mother passed. My mother went to meet her maker. My mother had gone on to her great reward. My mother had lost her battle. My mother had kicked the bucket. My mother had given up the ghost. My mother was pushing up daisies. My mother didn't make it. My mother was called home. I repeated these sentences to help it sink in while my body was still saying *nonononononononono*. Outside the air was thick with cicadas, I would have been alone without them.

I was born in the most northern of American towns with a clan of tall laughing aunts, uncles, a long-winded grandfather, a grandmother with long narrow hands, an absent father and a mysterious nothingness from his side of the family. I was born into big Christmas hams with pineapple slices on top and small sips of sparkling wine allowed and snowball fights in the woods. I was one in a spilling over of bodies, piled like puppies in the TV room. But I only ever belonged to one person—her, my mother. In the thin-walled shack, I imagined my mother's dead body floating near the ceiling, it was almost midnight. I forgot what it felt like to speak in a crowded room.

In Tuscaloosa a mockingbird floated over without flapping her wings, I made a wish against it. I thought of my northern childhood—shards of sharp snow patched the school yard. Once, when I was seven, I stood from kneeling amid the ice mud city I'd built, blood ran in ribbons down my legs striped across the white knee socks that had been clean that morning. My mother was always proud that I was clean. I came home from school, for once she wasn't playing the piano. She sat on the stoop in the gloaming around us. She was smoking, again. The quaking aspens were just where I'd left them with clean socks that morning. The sound of glass and gravel mixed under my shoe. The weak sinking sun caught the glass in her hair, a cut on her palm, a ridge of blue under one eye, her hand shook a little at the end of the red-tipped cigarette. A chair lay splintered. A window was broken. Somewhere water was running. I righted a table and pressed my face to the pillow. I felt something wet on my mouth and was surprised again by blood.

I read that grief is a hole you walk through
in the daytime and fall into at night.

The days were given shape with biscuits, walks in the morning and night, episodes of *Diners, Drive-Ins, and Dives*. I woke up hours before the ghost husband and tried each day to get the dog around the block for a walk. By 9am, it was already hot enough to make me whimper. The hummingbird lied still, lulled by my swaying walk. Sweat sprouted from unknown places. Belly and dog pulled me home like a kite on a string.

My hips unhinged for weeks and days past
the hummingbird's soft deadline I could feel
them threatening to pull me apart. I held
myself together by floating in the bath and
thinking about what I'd eat next.

I have never left meat on the bone. Long ago, I lost my first tooth gnawing on a chicken leg. In this one small way I felt at home in Tuscaloosa.

My mother was killed by men. She was killed by her own mother. She was killed by years of wanting to leave and feeling trapped. She was killed by iron and hot blood and a liver that hardened and backed up poison into her body, ammonia into her brain, yellow skin, bulging veins in her throat. She was killed by me, by my endless anger. She was killed by a tattoo at a biker party. She was killed by falling off a porch. She was killed by being born the first girl after a fistful of brothers. She was killed by the swirling pain in her brain and a need to become the moon.

I often thought of kicking the wall, throwing the dog, smashing a mug over the nearest head. Whether it was grief or pregnancy, I was loose like an unchained cannon. The ghost husband steered me toward the Target cashier least likely to comment on the size of my belly, least likely to say, "WOW! About to pop!" least likely to ask, "What are you having?" My rage was kept potent in the cauldron of my aching body.

When I was a girl my mother and I couldn't
agree on the color of salt. I held her under
the faucet of my rage. We pulled at each
other's guts cruelly, twisting and pinching
at each other.

The little dog yipped at the ghost hovering over a pan of spitting bacon in the kitchen and followed me out back through the bottle-cap yard to the magnolia tree. The sun was a hot iron on the part in my hair. I ducked under the greasy green leaves and waddled forward bent over awkwardly, the dog threatened to trip me and let out a soft whine. When we were both hidden in the tangled branches it felt good to be alone with my belly, the hummingbird, the sound of the wilting trumpet, and the furred cones littering the ground.

The rounder my belly got, the bigger the hummingbird, the more I found that I couldn't pull the meanings of words from the curves of my brain. The blurry edges of ideas and appointment times became thick as soup. I put lotion on my toothbrush. I recorded a nonsensical song on my phone because it was brilliant. I forgot what day I was born. In the thick of one melting afternoon the ghost came home and asked me what *antediluvian* meant. I had always been a source for meanings. I lolled on the couch and could only gesture toward my phone. He rippled with disappointment, and I saw him fade into something wholly transparent. *Between the fall of humans and the flood* was all I had to say but it's impossible to see where you are when you are in it.

My skin became a drum, the forces of gravity felt like a grave. There were tiny lead weights hooked into every inch of my skin. A hummingbird jumping in my belly.

I read about a missing man who joined the
search party for himself.

Before I left home, left my mother, I curdled
with lemon-peel bitterness. There is no
anger like puberty, savage like a tabby cat,
sad like a dandelion, grieving like a palisade.
My baby brother was a do-over. My face
turned into a dogfight, when I looked at it,
I felt an alarm. But the back of my face was
a place I could rest my hand. It was lonely
as my only witness. I testified daily but the
truth didn't seem to need an advocate.

When the ghost and I got to the hospital there were no beds. They were not expecting us. A nurse wheeled a bed into a storage closet until someone else gave birth and made room. The ghost and I ate from the same container of tender ribs, pulling the meat off the bone with greasy fingers. The ghost rippled with excitement about his dry rub, slow-roasted ribs. I couldn't taste anything except terror but devoured each morsel.

When I was a small child, my grandmother told me that when a baby dies without being baptized it is sentenced to the outermost ring of Hell called Limbo, a ring of flame slightly less hot than the Hell of the Damned. That was very possibly where we were in the hospital.

It's 4am in the hospital. I whisper to the ghost husband, *Are you awake?* There is no answer except for the roller coaster of contractions. I ask my dead mother, *Were you ever awake?* I never asked. I was told not to ask. *Where are you now, Mom? Do you see my window light reaching out to the street when you close your eyes? I see you small as a loaf of bread. I see you when you fit in my sock drawer. I see you when I close my eyes. I close my eyes. I close my eyes, you are still dead, still dead. Was I a picky eater? How old was I when I stopped wetting the bed?* I laid on the bed for weeks, or maybe it was years, or maybe it was just one night, holding the beach-ball belly, feeling for the moving hummingbird and all I can think about are the same handful: *Mother, Baby, Ghost.*

I labored for days and bled and flooded the room. I pushed for hours, and the baby could not come through. The ghost leaned in and whispered, "You are a badass bitch, and you can do this." But I couldn't.

I looked at the fresh boy, his skin on my skin. In the first days he never stopped frowning—wholly dissatisfied with the air and stink of earth. When the ghost lifted him from my arms, I felt my heavy body lighten and lift into the middle of the room. Messy hair tapped the cottage cheese ceiling, and I floated back down, a balloon without a string. *Mama* came out of my mouth. I was talking to us both. The little dog moved his head to my thigh, greedy for me now. *Mama, I didn't even like you most the time but where the fuck are you?* Rage simmered in me. A murmuration of starlings flew up from the yard. Somewhere near a bone snapped in half. The trumpet sound stumbled inside.

I felt a strong urge to call all my dead to tell them my mother had died. But, I remembered, you can't pick up a phone and talk to the dead.

There are straight-line winds in the woods where my mother lived. When I visited, I walked the woods for hours, and once in a wind storm the jack pines started crashing down around me in a lottery of terror. Jack pines topple as easily as blocks. They are long and thin and trap and kill. I ran home and tried to tell the story. Tornadoes don't go that far north. Dead foxes on the side of the road seemed to mean something.

My dead mother is a tooth under my scalp,
a bone buried in my skeleton.

I meant to tell my mother some things: An octopus can go anywhere her tentacle can go. A cat can go no wider than her whiskers. A mouse can go anywhere his head will fit. I wear black in the daytime to camouflage myself against tall buildings. My body wrung itself out to make a person and now it's stretched out and flaps around me like nervous hands.

Years ago, a woman on the bus said her god was the wind because she could feel it but never see it. My heart said *bullshit*, I thought of tornadoes. The wind has always been my enemy.

My mother said she would write her own story one day, her version of her life. In our thin-walled shack in Tuscaloosa I spent most afternoons alone. I stood naked on a stool in front of the bathroom mirror to get the full effect of my new shape. I looked for my mother's ghost behind my eyes, I imagined chastising her, "You didn't get the chance to write your story because you are so fucking stupid that you died." The hummingbird baby kicked at my rage. I stepped down and made us a sandwich.

Before the hummingbird I could only think about the ghost. I wrapped my legs around the waist of the night. Embarrassed at my own enthusiasm for things I never wanted, like the word *boyfriend* which was like calling the sun a 60-watt bulb. Likewise, *I love you, I miss you.* The hedonism of wanting the ghost with such primitive need soured my stomach. In those early months it was all I could do to walk in the morning, ignoring the little dog who only wanted me and no one else.

I put zinnias in a blue jar with a little sugar water. A small jolt of joy when I passed them on the table. The ghost put beautiful plates of food on the table and called for me, "It's time to eat!"

There were starlings nesting in the eaves of the thin-walled Tuscaloosa house. They screamed and shit all day. Nothing could be done. I wandered outside and found a dead bird crawling with ants and sat beside it to watch death and industry in the dappled shade of the magnolia.

I want to tell my mother, *A man sat too close to me on the train. He snaked his hand along my thigh and squeezed, touched himself and touched me. I can't even do handstands in my yard without getting advice. I tell you this, so you know you have a woman out in the world. Sometimes I stand over the sink, eating a plum, looking at nothing. I am okay above the white porcelain.*

I start writing letters to the fresh boy in my mind, I tell him, *I want to ask you to give me all the possibility you've got.*

I was born in the driftless zone—a great yawn of land where the icebergs had split and spared the subtle sloping valleys. It was in those northern hollows that I grew into the shape of my mother. I grew and grew, sometimes with my grandmother on a bluff in a yellow house and sometimes with my young mother in a singlewide dented by long winters. I had the north in my lungs. I had the north embedded in my skin and in my ears the call of the common loon. Nothing could feel cold after that. North country girl. I learned how to harvest wild ramps without killing them and how to crouch in creeks hunting for watercress. I learned to skateboard barefoot and how to drink a 40oz Mickey's and not fall into the Mississippi River. This was where I felt pulled in the weeks after my mother died.

In the year before I joined the ghost in Alabama, I spent all my money on airline tickets. I flew to him over and over through the air and in my dreams. Once I woke up on an airplane flying over Memphis. I pulled the shade to let the light in over the city that raised him. I mouthed the words to that poem.

"If this were Tennessee and across that river, Arkansas, I'd meet you in West Memphis tonight. We could have a big time."

I thought for a moment about those poor boys, the West Memphis Three, the dirt and sadness, the ravaged bodies of babies. Then, I thought about that night I rode across that river with the ghost at the wheel, looking for gar. Looking for Frank Stanford, looking for the thick southern light that flickered in his chest. The ghost said something about the Mississippi River being the place where we were both at home. I grew up on the upper half, he grew up on the lower half. On the airplane, my wristwatch reminded me of how far in space and time I lived from my beloved ghost—who wasn't yet a

ghost. My heartbeat snuck forward, toward
him. I landed in the dirty south in the late
afternoon. *I'll swim to you*, I murmured.
Soon, I had the ghost's hand on my knee.
He always had a cold glass of something
waiting for me. He let my tired body rest
at his kitchen table, piled with books. We
agreed to break each other's hearts at some
later date.

A woman crossed the street to exclaim at me
in the melting Tuscaloosa heat.

She said, "Oooooh! A May baby!"

I said, "No."

"June?"

"July."

She crossed the street.

In the darkest room of the thin-walled shack, I curled around the hummingbird and started to suspect that I didn't exist. I believed for a time that all the light of the world was coming from my own eyes. When I went to the place in the back of my head where I was only witnessing the play of images and fragments of people around me—I put on the ghost's favorite shirt and pulled my selves back inside. I tried to recall where he put his hands on my body before the hummingbird dwelled inside. I thought of being given back to the pull of gravity, the last time he set me down.

My mother and I were the same kind of fugitive pieces having passed through the void of cities with the same eyes. When she stopped to die, in the boiling heat—I wanted her to know that she and I were two flat rocks skipping across the same black water.

Years before she died, I went to see her
after she had her first heart attack. We sat
together in the high captain chairs of her
truck. I was in the driver's seat, the leather
pressed close to the steering wheel. She
spread her square hands into stars on the
dash. A sigh and I knew she had a confession
to make—a sequence of events she needed
to arrange for me. I stared forward into the
north woods while she set the scene, thirty
years before, 21 years old and homeless
with a baby; a wicked ex-sister-in-law, a
small cocaine habit, a feeling of isolation,
and a terrible argument. Somehow, she
wound up—these words have been applied
so liberally—*somehow*, she wound up
wandering the streets of Denver with a small
bag, a medium-sized baby, and nowhere to
go. *Somehow*, she wound up in a four-season
porch with a small cardboard box for a crib
in a house of long-haired bikers. *Somehow*,
she wound up leaving the baby, just for an
hour to have a beer at the tavern down the
hill. *Somehow*, she wound up being beaten
in the parking lot by a pack of women
screaming that she had left her baby alone.
Somehow, she wound up bleeding and

crying on the four-season porch, but quietly because the baby was sleeping. *Somehow*, she wound up talking to the police, they didn't mind that she had been beaten. *Somehow*, she wound up watching the lady-cop gently pick the baby up and carry her away. *Somehow*, I spent nine months being taken care of by strangers.

In the weeks after my mother's death, I was savage like the tilting lupine leaching the soil with my woody root. Nothing grew near me, only the hummingbird continued to thrive, I was a wolf wrapped in a cone of petals. My snout was covered in gilded pollen. I trampled the sweet sprout of the ghost's hand reaching for mine. That summer, I devoured all the tender grasses. My only desire was to ravage, to loot and forage and revile. In those early days I was not okay. Also, I had to be okay. I had to be okay for the ghost and for the hummingbird moving in my belly. I got dressed each day, answered my phone when it rang, checked the mail, hefted the recycling outside, made dinner, threw a goodbye party for myself, smiled for several photographs, fraudulently applied for unemployment, went for long walks with friends, moved across the country to be with the ghost who was also my husband and father of the hummingbird.

In one of my childhood houses, a house which wasn't a house at all, except for the walls and blue rough-cut carpet that I didn't know to call *shag*. My mother came home flushed and chattering with a new red sweatsuit on, her tan articulated hands pulling things from a bag. Parcheesi, the only game we would ever play, came that day. She asked if I knew the meaning of *baby*, as in younger and from her. Then, the idea was forgotten, the baby dropped into that house, as quickly as it had rushed in like the birds against the windows that were too clean or big or closed, it fell to the ground. No one said *abortion* until decades later. Unlike the birds, I didn't pick the idea of the baby up and keep it in my closet in a birdcage. I didn't look for it in the cupboards of that house, as I looked for proof that there was no man coming to save us with gifts. In that house my Christmas gift was a Fievel doll wrapped in tinfoil and a five-dollar bill folded like a bow tie. In that house I hid things and talked in my sleep. I gathered rocks and made kites. In that house she stayed in her red sweatsuit for days, crying on the couch.

A black dog with mange and a beaver tail of dreadlock limped into our yard and lay at my mother's feet. She said, "This is Oliver," and so he was. My mother refused to visit my dreams, but Oliver trotted through several times. I woke up and told her ghost in case it was there in the room at the end of the bed, "The sun has no ownership over the moon, but you can't tell the moon that." I knew she'd get it.

My pregnant body grew into the bed, and we became one. I guiltily dreamed about sleeping on my back. My little dog curled his long, odd mutt body around the bowl of belly that held the hummingbird. As the hummingbird grew the little dog's eyes got wider and his fur started to fall out in great clumps. He whined and I rolled my distended body out to the back porch where I sat painfully on the rickety steps in my underwear and tossed a ball. This little dog I'd once cherished disappeared under the porch and returned covered with motor oil. He slipped past me and ran into the little sloped house, rolling on the white carpets and shimmying under the new couch. Oil everywhere. I lumbered after him screaming and cursing, I squatted low, my Olympic-sized swimming pool belly hanging down threatening to split and spill, and dragged him out by his haunches, sweeping his grease-covered body up and against me in a slick embrace. He made several successful escapes, but I always found him again.

I'd been accused of laughing when I should be crying. I came by it naturally. My grandmother had ten children but along with all that birth death soon followed. The oldest, Timmy, was killed by a drunk driver at 2pm in the afternoon. He was checking the mail, it was a warm day in March, he was nine. She found his teeth in the grass, she said he had the most beautiful teeth. Two babies died after that in cribs as babies sometimes do. Another son went mad. Another son went to war and came back angry and drunk. Another son lost himself to drugs. The girls were pummeled by rape, by incest, by their own inefficient bodies. I was raised in this grief.

You've been dead for two months. I had been bouncing on a yoga ball for days to try to get the baby to come. I was covered in stretch marks and my face grew round and full. The veins in my body were throbbing and when I walked, I felt like I could fall apart and tumble to the ground. When I leaned forward in Downward Dog, beads of colostrum bloomed from my nipples. Fighting to walk and breathe and sleep showed me the love she had for me, too late.

I didn't want the nurses to wash the baby boy after he was born, something I'd read about microbiomes and the healing power of vernix. I wanted to keep my placenta too. The nurse said, "I know which baby is yours, he's the dirty one." They put my placenta in a biohazard bag at the foot of my bed. The ghost took it home and put it in the freezer so I could eat it later. He brought me a cheeseburger and a chocolate milkshake. It felt good to eat without guilt one last time. For five days I was sealed in a room, they wouldn't release me until I could take a shit. I stood in the shower and lightly felt my incision. I had been stapled shut. My wound screamed but I felt almost nothing. I shuffled up and down the halls. I stared at the tiny bundle next to my bed. I felt around in the dark for something that wasn't there.

.

ACKNOWLEDGMENTS

I would like to thank the many people who helped birth this book.

First and foremost, Grant Gerald Miller, my husband and father of the boy, who was generous and unflagging in his support of this work.

My publisher Greg Gerding and editor John Barrios for their investment and patience.

To all the writers and readers who gave me feedback over the years including Justin Hocking, Mesha Maren, Megan Kruse, and Suzanne Lunden Metzger.

Thank you to Maxwell Gerald Miller, my son, for giving me new reasons to be alive. I love you beyond all reason.

Lastly, thank you to the town of Tuscaloosa which will aways be the place I became a mother. Roll Tide Roll.

AUTHOR BIO

A.M. O'Malley is a writer and visual artist who has been published in *Newer York*, *Nailed Magazine*, *The Nervous Breakdown*, *Jerkpoet*, *Poor Claudia*, *Burnside Review*, *Fog Machine*, and *Portland Review*. O'Malley's first full-length book of hybrid poem-memoir *Expecting Something Else* was published by University of Hell Press in 2016. This is her second full-length book. O'Malley lives in Nashville, Tennessee, with her husband, writer and photographer, Grant Gerald Miller, and their son, Max.

www.ingramcontent.com/pod-product-compliance
Lightning Source LLC
Chambersburg PA
CBHW041929090426
42744CB00016B/1993